LILLIAN TOO'S
LITTLE BOOK OF
FENg
SHUI
风水
AT WORK

Lillian Too's Little Book of Feng Shui at Work

Lillian Too

ELEMENT

Shaftesbury, Dorset • Boston, Massachusetts
Melbourne, Victoria

© Element Books Limited 1999
Text © Lillian Too 1999

First published in the UK in 1999 by
Element Books Limited
Shaftesbury, Dorset SP7 8BP

Published in the USA in 1999 by
Element Books, Inc.
160 North Washington Street
Boston, MA 02114

Published in Australia in 1999 by
Element Books and distributed
by Penguin Australia Limited
487 Maroondah Highway, Ringwood,
Victoria 3134

Cover design by Mark Slader
Design and typesetting by Drum Enterprises Ltd
Printed and bound by Bemrose Security Printing, Derby

British Library Cataloguing in Publication data available

Library of Congress Cataloging in Publication data available

ISBN 1 86204 585 2

For Jennifer, now more than ever.

INTRODUCTION

Use the tips in this little book to create an auspicious environment at your workplace. As well as guidelines on how to arrange the furniture, where to sit and which colours to wear, there is information on lucky symbols you can display to enhance your position and promote business success. Equally important, there is advice on what situations and features to avoid.

Feng shui can truly help you to harness the positive energies that reinforce good career luck. It costs you nothing to try . . .

Lillian Too

Always Sit Facing
The Door

If you have your back to the door, you could be betrayed, cheated, or stabbed in the back. Good work luck is completely missing.

FIND THE POWER SPOT IN YOUR OFFICE

The best location for your desk is the far corner diagonal to the entrance. This is the power spot in any office and is most auspicious.

Sit With Your Back To The Wall

Having a solid wall behind you gives important back support. Without this you are sure to lose out in office politics. You will also lose the support of your bosses.

HANG A MOUNTAIN BEHIND YOU

During bad times, strengthen the support behind you by hanging a picture of a mountain on the wall behind your chair. Try a picture of Mount Everest!

ENERGIZE THE TURTLE
SYMBOL

The turtle will ensure long-term and successful employment. Place a real turtle or a picture of this celestial creature at your back to represent stability of tenure.

Turn Your Shelves
Into Cupboards

Get rid of exposed open shelves that may be
sending knife-like vibrations towards you.
Make them into cupboards by installing
doors.

Block Wall Edges With Flowers Or Plants

Place flowers or a small plant on your desk so that they are between you and any corner wall or pillar edge that may be sending poisonous breath your way. Ensure they are fresh and change them frequently.

Do Not Sit Facing A Pillar

Never have a pillar directly in front of you;
this blocks your progress at work. If possible
re-orientate your desk so that the pillar is
behind you.

SIMULATE A
BRIGHT HALL

If you sit facing a wall, decorate it with
prints showing either a wide-open field or a
water scene. This simulates an auspicious
'bright hall' and taps the feng shui luck of
the symbolic water.

KEEP CACTI OUT OF THE OFFICE

Do not embellish window ledges or tables with cactus plants. Their thorns are tiny arrows that cause bad luck to build up and eventually hurt you.

BLOCK OUT
INAUSPICIOUS VIEWS

Use curtains or blinds to block out unsightly
views such as the sharp edge of another
building.

WATCH OUT FOR OVERHEAD BEAMS

Do not sit directly below an exposed overhead beam – either move away from it or hang a five-rod wind chime from the edge of the beam to correct this very bad feature.

NEVER HANG A PA KUA INSIDE

A Pa Kua (an eight-sided protective symbol) can be extremely harmful when hung indoors so it is important to remove any that may have been hung by someone else. Despite what you may have been told, never hang a Pa Kua mirror anywhere inside your office or workplace.

AVOID SITTING AT THE END
OF A LONG CORRIDOR

Try not to sit or have your desk at the end of
a long corridor – this location is inauspicious.
If there is no alternative, hang bright lights at
the entrance to the corridor.

DISPLAY
SOMETHING RED

Give your career a boost with something red
- a painting or a curtain - or place a red
light on the south wall of your room. This
will speed up recognition of your efforts.

CREATE A WATER FEATURE IN THE NORTH

A water feature in your office will bring excellent career luck – but don't overdo it. Too much water could drown you! Always keep the water clean.

Place Plants In The Southeast

In any room of the workplace plants in this location enhance income luck. Fake plants are as effective as real plants, but never use dried plants or arrangements. These emit unlucky energies.

Don't Let Your Files Block You

Never allow files to pile up directly in front of you on your desk. If your desk-top is usually stacked high with files, place them on either side and leave the centre part of your desk clear.

MAINTAIN YIN/YANG BALANCE IN YOUR OFFICE

Yin, receptive energy, is cool and passive; yang, creative energy, is bright and active. Workplaces that are dominated by 'grey' could be excessively yin – introduce some yang energy with plants or colourful paintings.

ATTRACT YANG ENERGY WITH LIGHTS

Keep your workplace well lit and bright. This attracts yang energy, which brings exceedingly good luck. Yang energy is especially important during winter months when days are short and nights are long.

HANG UP A CRYSTAL TO DIFFUSE EXCESSIVE YANG ENERGY

If your workplace suffers from too much yang energy caused by, say, the strength of the afternoon sun on a west-oriented window, hang a faceted crystal to break up the rays and create a happy rainbow of coloured lights.

IMPROVE IRREGULAR-SHAPED OFFICES WITH MIRRORS

Regular-shaped work spaces are best – if yours is irregular, use lights to brighten tight corners or wall mirrors to regularize the shape.

REDUCE CLUTTER TO ENCOURAGE HARMONY

Do not allow your work space to get untidy or dirty. Clutter is often a cause of misunderstandings and disharmony among colleagues.

CREATE CURVED
TRAFFIC FLOWS

Allowing the chi to meander promotes
harmony in the workplace. Encourage this in
the arrangement of desks and dividers in an
open-plan office.

AVOID CONFRONTATIONAL
SEATING ARRANGEMENTS

When people sit directly facing each other
office politics will become unbearable and
disruptive. Workers should never sit facing
each other in a confrontational mode.

DISSOLVE THE 'KILLING ENERGY' OF SQUARE PILLARS

Place plants, especially creepers, in front of the edges of square pillars to dissolve dangerous energies. Change these plants every three months as dying plants cause misfortune.

HANG A SIX-ROD WINDCHIME IN THE NORTHWEST

In this corner of your office or allocated work space, a windchime will attract the notice and support of your boss.

'Feng Shui' Your Desk

Divide the surface into nine equal sections and use a compass to mark each one with its corresponding direction. The centre is left empty.

- Place some flowers, a small leafy plant or a green-coloured object in the east or southeast for success and prosperity.

- Place something blue in the north to activate career luck.

- Place your computer, your telephone or your calculator in the northwest or west for the luck of powerful friends and influential mentors.

- Place a bright tablelamp in the south to enhance your chances of promotion, or place a decorative bird - preferably the phoenix - here to attract lucrative career opportunities.

- Place a smooth crystal ball in the southwest to ensure pleasant and congenial relationships with your subordinates, colleagues and peers.

- Place a crystal or globe in the northeast to enhance personal development.

PLACE CASH REGISTERS IN THE SOUTHEAST FOR ADDED INCOME

All retail establishments benefit from having the cash register placed in the income corner (southeast) of the shop.

Keep The Front Of Your Desktop Clear

Irrespective of what direction it represents, always keep the space directly in front of you empty of files, objects or any energizers. Anything placed here will symbolically block your luck.

AVOID SITTING IN FRONT OF A TOILET WALL

When a toilet is on the other side of the wall behind you, all your career plans and work will count for nothing. Move your desk away from this position.

CHECK OUT THE LAYOUT OF THE FLOOR ABOVE

If you find your work space is beneath a toilet, try to change the orientation and location of your desk so that you are not directly beneath this inauspicious feature.

RAISE THE ENERGY IN A LOW-CEILINGED OFFICE

If you get a feeling of being hemmed in and cramped, installing bright lights and using white paint to raise the energy is a good solution.

DISPLAY EARTH ELEMENT OBJECTS

If you work in the property business, displaying a cluster of natural quartz crystal, decorative stones, a wall map of the world or a painting of mountains is auspicious.

Incorporate Feng Shui In The Design Of Restaurants

Restaurants benefit hugely from mirrors and water motifs. Colour schemes can range from blue to black. Lighting should not be too bright or too dim.

ENERGIZE YOUR SHOP TO ATTRACT MORE CUSTOMERS

Fine jewellery boutiques benefit from mirrors and bright light. Placing decorative crystals among the pieces will also attract more customers into the shop.

Hang Wall Mirrors To Double Your Sales

Floor-to-ceiling wall mirrors in shops tend to double the number of customers and product lines, and are thus very good for business.

INSTALL AN AQUARIUM TO ENERGIZE TURNOVER LUCK

To enhance sales install a bubbling aquarium in the north, east or southeast corner of a shop. Shine bright lights directly into the aquarium and watch the shadows move continuously on the ceiling above.

INVITE PROSPERITY WITH CHINESE COINS

Paste three Chinese coins – yang side up and tied with auspicious red thread – onto cash registers, money boxes and invoice books to embellish business luck.

PLACE IMAGES OF WATER IN FRONT OF YOU

Never have a picture of water behind you –
scenes showing rivers, waterfalls and lakes
should always hang in front of you, never at
your back. Water behind always symbolizes
missed opportunities.

NEVER HAVE MOUNTAINS IN FRONT OF YOU

Images of hills, mountains and big buildings should never be hung directly facing you. This symbolizes confronting the mountain, and obstacles will block the success of your plans.

BEWARE OF DOORS IN A STRAIGHT LINE

If there are three doors in a straight line, keep the centre door closed at all times.

CREATE A SPACIOUS FOYER TO BRING GOOD LUCK

An office with a reception area tends to have better feng shui because it allows chi to accumulate. Keep this area well lit and fortified with precious yang energy.

ENSURE YOUR ENTRANCE DOOR IS SOLID

A solid door is preferable to a glass door. However, a glass door that opens onto the reception area with a solid wall facing the entrance compensates for the absence of a solid door.

DISPLAY A SAILING SHIP FOR EXCELLENT BUSINESS LUCK

An excellent tip for greatly enhancing profits is to display a ship symbolically sailing into harbour loaded to the brim with gold. Make sure the ship faces inwards, never outwards.

Hang Bells On Door Handles

A small bell on the door handle outside any retail shop encourages customers to enter. Directing them past the cash register via a meandering pathway entices them to purchase something.

MAKE YOUR BUSINESS CARDS AUSPICIOUS

Choose a corporate logo that incorporates good fortune symbols. The dragon is one of the luckiest symbols to use, especially if you make it look fat and pregnant!

INTRODUCE PRECIOUS YANG ENERGY INTO A DULL OFFICE

To improve the feng shui of a drab-looking office, use colourful blinds, hang a painting, play some music or get the office repainted. Yang should always dominate, but never to the total exclusion of yin. Keep the balance.

Don't Let The Energies Of Your Workplace Stagnate

Open the windows and doors of your office to let the energies flow. Offices that are heated through the winter or air-conditioned throughout the year will benefit from fresh air and sunshine.

MAKE AND KEEP A WEALTH WALLET IN YOUR DRAWER

Place three Chinese coins tied with red thread, and some hard currency inside your symbolic wealth wallet. Add a small amount of soil taken from a rich man's home (keep it in a plastic bag).

ENERGIZE IMPORTANT FILES

Stick coins, good luck calligraphy symbols or pictures of the auspicious dragon or turtle on the covers of important contracts and files.

ASSESS THE FENG SHUI OF YOUR OFFICE BUILDING

Look out for sharp, straight or hostile
structures that are aimed at the main
entrance of your building. Deflect these with
a Pa Kua mirror hung above the entrance.

CHECK THE CONTOURS OF THE LAND AROUND YOUR OFFICE

Make certain that land at the back of your building is higher or on the same level as land in the front of the building.

ALWAYS ENTER BY THE MAIN FRONT DOOR

Enter your workplace each morning via the main entrance into the building. This is especially recommended if the orientation of the building is auspicious. Use a side door only when poison arrows afflict the main door.

Calculate Your Kua Number
To Discover Your Personal
Auspicious Directions

Add together the last two digits of your year
of birth and keep adding until reduced to a
single digit. Then, add 5 if you are female
(and add together again if the number is
more than one digit) or deduct from 10 if
you are a male. The result is your Kua
number.

East group people have Kua numbers 1, 3, 4 or 9. Your four auspicious directions are east, southeast, north and south so always remember to sit facing these directions. Never use west group directions.

West group people have Kua numbers 2, 5, 6, 7 or 8. Your auspicious directions are west, southwest, northwest and northeast. Use them in many different ways to bring good luck. Never use east group directions.

SELECT JOB INTERVIEW CLOTHES TO MATCH YOUR KUA NUMBER

Here are the luckiest colours for each of the Kua numbers. For 1 wear dark blue; for 2 and 8 wear beige or cream; for 3 and 4 wear green; for 6 and 7 wear white; and for 9 wear any shade of red.

APPLY YOUR KUA NUMBER WHEN TRAVELLING ON BUSINESS

You will receive good luck when you travel from one of your auspicious directions. For example: travelling from the UK to the USA (that is, from the northeast) is better for west than for east group people.

CHECK OUT THE KUA NUMBERS OF YOUR COLLEAGUES

People of the same group, east or west, tend to be more compatible. If working with people from the opposite group, you will need to work harder at the relationship.

Sit In The Right Direction To Attract Good Luck

When you sit facing one of the lucky directions in your group (east or west), opportunities and promotion will come your way. To sit facing a direction belonging to the other group will be unlucky for you.

CHECK WHICH DIRECTION YOUR MAIN ENTRANCE FACES

If the main entrance of your workplace opens out to any one of the four directions in your group you will enjoy good feng shui at work. If it faces any one of the directions in the other group, your work will give you little satisfaction.

Wear Green When You Need Confidence

Personal feng shui starts with the colours and the cut of the clothes you wear as well as how you wear them. Green stands for strong growth energy.

WEAR BRIGHT REDS, YELLOWS AND ORANGES TO CREATE PRECIOUS YANG ENERGY

Clothes in these colours are excellent when you lack confidence. Red gives strength and is itself an auspicious colour. Wear it to get noticed.

Wear Blacks And Blues To Cool Down Excessive Enthusiasm And Zeal

Clothes in these colours are effective when summer days get too hot or when tempers get frayed due to excessive work loads. Always have a dark-blue jacket ready. It can be reassuring to fling it over you for protection when pressure mounts.

WEAR WHITE FOR INCREASED AUTHORITY

To become more assertive and authoritative, nothing works better than wearing white. It is especially effective when combined with a gold brooch or a silver pin because the metal element generates an aura of power and authority.

CHOOSE FIRE COLOURS FOR A SALES OR PR FUNCTION

Bright red attracts recognition and respect. Reds are lucky all year round, but especially during winter when they create much needed yang energy.

ENERGIZE YOUR
LEADERSHIP QUALITIES

During management or budget meetings,
activate the metallic chi of the creative *chien*
trigram. Wear white and put on some gold
jewellery or accessories. Men can wear gold
cufflinks.

ACTIVATE YOUR FAX MACHINE

Bring good feng shui into the office by orientating the machine so that faxes come from one of your auspicious directions. Also, attach three Chinese coins, tied together with red thread, to the fax machine.

CHOOSE YOUR BRIEFCASE
WITH CARE

Briefcases can be made of any material. Black
is best. In feng shui black symbolizes income
and money, and when black is combined
with metal, the symbolism created is
auspicious and harmonious. So look for
metallic clasps – and do choose black.

HANG DIPLOMAS, AWARDS AND CERTIFICATES TO YOUR LEFT SIDE

If you do this you will go from strength to strength. Do not place these evidences of your achievements near toilets or where they will be hit by a sharp wall edge.

DO NOT DISPLAY PLANTS WITH SHARP, POINTED OR LONG LEAVES

If in doubt, go for rounded leaves or, better still, go for plants with round succulent leaves. These are particularly auspicious. Do not let your plants get spindly and sickly, if they become weak throw them out and replace them with new ones.

RELIEVE PHYSICAL TENSIONS WITH A SIMPLE CHI EXERCISE

Stand with feet apart, slowly bend your knees as though sitting on an imaginary chair. Keep your back straight and head erect. Place hands parallel to the ground and at 90 degrees to your body. Flex palms upwards 90 degrees. Hold . . . and feel the chi.

CALM YOUR ANGER BY TAKING SLOW, DEEP BREATHS

Watch your breath as you take it slowly into your abdomen. Hold for three seconds and then very, very slowly, let the breath out. This 'yin breathing' will soothe you instantly if you become angry at work.

ENERGIZE YOURSELF WITH YANG BREATHING

Practise this exercise before an important presentation. Breathe in deeply and hold for three seconds, then breathe out in strong short spurts. Let your muscles tense and then let them go, relaxing completely. Do this three times. If you concentrate during this breathing exercise you will raise auspicious chi.

HOLD MEETINGS AT ROUND TABLES

Meetings held at round tables tend to be smooth and without obstacles, especially when held in west-facing rooms. Round tables create good relationships and foster teamwork so the best decisions are made and goodwill flourishes.

OR, SIT AT A LONG
RECTANGULAR TABLE

Long rectangular tables symbolize growth
and can also be auspicious. But beware of
two potential dangers. To sit at a corner with
the table edge pointing towards your
stomach is extreme misfortune. These same
corner edges also send out killing energy.

NEVER INSTALL GLASS FURNITURE

See-through glass or perspex tables are bad
news as they represent a lack of support and
cause immense unpopularity. Switch to solid
wood, especially a solid hardwood as it
represents healthy and solid growth.

Choose Chairs With Solid Back Supports And Armrests

Chairs (and sofas) with low backs and no armrests are completely inauspicious. You will become unpopular and isolated.

REMEMBER THAT METAL DESTROYS WOOD IN FENG SHUI

So nails in furniture create discordant energies. Furniture that is joined without nails is the most auspicious. Think of those seamless and beautifully curved antique Ming chairs – so auspicious!

USE LIGHTING TO ATTRACT GOOD ENERGY

Lights – with the exception of spotlights – solve a variety of feng shui problems; they dissolve the killing chi of hidden arrows and enhance yang energy. Keep your office foyer and your desk well lit at all times.

CREATE HARMONY
WITH LIGHT

Yellow light in the southwest and northeast and white light in the northwest and west will create exceptionally harmonious flows in the workplace. They are very conducive to the fostering of goodwill.

BENEFIT FROM THE GROWTH ENERGY OF THE EAST AND SOUTHEAST

Sit in these corners of the office if you are an ambitious, workaholic type who is eager to put in 16-hour days.

LOCATE YOURSELF IN THE WEST WHEN NEARING RETIREMENT

If you want to slow down your pace of work sit in the west. This is the place of the setting sun – symbolic of yin getting stronger. You will retire gracefully here.

SIT IN THE NORTHWEST IF YOU'RE THE BOSS

Chief executives are best here as this is the place of the *chien* trigram, symbolic of the leader. Hang a six-rod wind chime to maintain your strength and luck.

DO NOT HAVE A BRIGHT LIGHT SHINING BEHIND YOU

If there is a bright light behind your seat, try to dim it. Fire behind suggests betrayal and people cheating you. In a power struggle within the company, you will surely lose.

Broaden Narrow Hallways With Wall Mirrors

You could also slow down the flow of chi with small plants if there is sufficient space, or hang pictures of landscapes to add depth.

HANG THE COMPANY FOUNDER'S PICTURE ON THE NORTHWEST WALL

If hung anywhere else the portrait of the founder will cause bad luck for the company, especially if he or she is already dead. In the northwest their picture will create good luck.

ENERGIZE THE SOUTHWEST TO MAXIMIZE FEMALE POWER

If the founder is a woman, hang her portrait in the southwest of the office. This is the place of the matriarch and women in this location will bring exceptional benefits to the company.

ENERGIZE YOUR PREMISES WITH REVOLVING DOORS

Revolving doors tend to be auspicious because they allow the chi energy entering the building to stay fresh and stimulated. They are also an excellent way of deflecting and dissolving any bad energy aimed at the entrance.

PUT YOUR NAME UP THERE!

Signboards of any business – corporate or retail – should be hung higher than the door. If you put the name of your business lower down, it suggests an inability to prosper.

Ensure That Any Water Flows Towards The Main Entrance

When water flows away from a building it carries the company's finances with it. Fountains have a neutral effect.

PERFORM A PURIFICATION RITUAL BEFORE TRAVELLING ON BUSINESS

If you anticipate a tough trip, do the following to create good feng shui:

- Light a candle if travelling west or northwest.
- Slice the air with a curved knife if travelling east or southeast.
- Plant a tree if travelling southwest or northeast.
- Throw a bucket of water towards the direction of travel if going south.
- Burn some incense if travelling north.

MAXIMIZE THE LUCK
CREATED BY HIGH CEILINGS

High ceilings symbolize growth energy.
However they are lucky only as long as there
are no sharp corners created in ceiling
design or exposed overhead or structural
beams.

ENHANCE THE FENG SHUI
OF MEETING ROOMS AND
BOARDROOMS

Balanced feng shui in these rooms is
achieved by the presence of all five elements
- a plant, white walls, a water feature, a
decorative crystal and well-lit interiors. The
elements can be combined in different ways,
but all five should be present.

ENSURE THAT STAIRCASES
HAVE SOLID STEPS

If they don't, money escapes. If a staircase
directly faces the entrance, either hang a very
bright light between the stairs and the door,
hang a five-rod windchime or turn the last
three steps of the staircase.

Incorporate The Colours Purple And Silver

This very auspicious combination of colours symbolically represents money. Other excellent combinations are blue with green, and red with gold. Use these auspicious colour combinations in your business.

DON'T THROW OUT YOUR L-SHAPED DESKS!

Unlike L-shaped rooms, L-shaped desks are not a problem in feng shui. Treat the desk as two separate tables and energize both according to the compass. But make sure you sit facing your correct direction. Mark it out with an arrow.

STRENGTHEN EARTH ENERGY FOR EXTRA LUCK

If you sit in the centre of an open-plan office, place a natural crystal cluster on your desk. Or place a small rock tied with red string under your table.

HANG BAMBOO RODS ABOVE CABINETS AND ON BEAMS

Bamboo rods activated with red thread are an auspicious feature for the office as they stimulate the qualities inherent in bamboo - strength, resilience and longevity.

Do Not Place A Clock Directly Opposite The Main Entrance

Clocks have negative connotations and the bad effect is compounded if they are shaped like a Pa Kua – they will drive business away.

DISPLAY A LUCKY MONEY CAT

This Japanese symbol of good business luck attracts money into the office. Place one on a table facing the main entrance into the office. Lucky money cats are white with gold and black markings.

STIMULATE YOUR
NETWORKING LUCK

Try activating the northwest portion of your
desktop by placing a small metallic bell in
this corner, or find a natural quartz crystal
cluster to place here. In addition, wear white
more often. These methods are also good for
improving your relationship with your boss.

ENLARGE CRAMPED SPACES AND SMALL ROOMS WITH WALL MIRRORS

Do not use mirror tiles and make sure that the mirrored wall does not face a door, a window, a staircase or a toilet.

KEEP ANTIQUE FURNITURE OUT OF THE WORKPLACE

One can never be sure of the provenance of old furniture, and since negative yin energies tend to cling to such old pieces, they are usually not good for careers or business.

CHOOSE YOUR
SCREEN SAVER CAREFULLY

Your computer screen will not hurt you, but
do take account of feng shui when
configuring your screen saver or when
downloading wallpaper. Do not let a fierce
panther stare out of your monitor; he could
symbolically 'hurt' you.

Hang A Pa Kua Mirror Outside To Avoid Extreme Bad Luck

If the entrance to your office faces a T-junction, or there is any other offending structure projecting poison arrows towards the building, place a Pa Kua mirror *outside* above the centre of the entrance to ward off the shar chi.

Avoid Triangular Or Abstract Designs In Paintings

Images with sharp, pointed features are hostile in the office. They carry secret poison arrows that harm. Remove all such works of art before they cause you grief.

POWER YOUR COMPUTER NOTEBOOK FROM AN AUSPICIOUS DIRECTION

This will ensure a happy relationship between you and your laptop because you will be tapping your auspicious direction.

Never Send Red Flowers To The Boss

Not even on her birthday. Red flowers are not associated with good fortune. Instead choose yellow blooms for your bouquets as these will bring good fortune.

Place A Plant In The East Or Southeast Corner

A small jade tree and money plants particularly attract greater prosperity into your career. Refrain from displaying any plants with thin, long leaves, and always remove plants as soon as they fade or shrivel up.

DISPLAY SPECIAL PLANTS
AT NEW YEAR

Choose two large potted lime plants for your office. They should be heavy with fruit since such symbols bring enormous New Year luck. If limes are not available, oranges, peaches and lemons can be good substitutes.

Place A Pot Of Flowering Narcissi On Your Desk At New Year

This symbolizes the flowering of your hidden talents in the coming year and creates excellent career luck for the future.

Do Not Hang Pictures Of Wild Animals In Your Office

Only those born in tiger and dragon years can withstand the presence of a tiger in their workplace. Those born in a small animal year should pay particular heed to this advice! So check your Chinese astrology.

BALANCE THE MALE AND FEMALE ENERGIES IN YOUR WORK SPACE

Offices that are overly feminine lack the assertive yang force, and workplaces that are excessively masculine often suffer from an overdose of yang energy. Stay balanced!

WORK
WITH MUSIC

Pleasant sounds imbue the surrounding
environment with gently flowing yang
energy that creates harmony.

POSITION YOUR FILING CABINET WHERE IT CANNOT HURT YOU

If a steel filing cabinet is behind you, it can send hidden arrows towards your back, especially if an edge directly aims at your back. Place it elsewhere.

KEEP A DRAGON FISH IN YOUR OFFICE

If you want to create serious wealth luck in your workplace, consider keeping a single arrowana fish near the entrance. Let it grow as big as possible; when its scales turn pink or gold it is an indication of impending wealth.

DISPLAY AUSPICIOUS CHINESE CALLIGRAPHY

Almost all successful Chinese offices display auspicious calligraphy. A popular word is the Chinese character 'fook', which means 'luck'. Some people believe that hanging this character upside down will increase business turnover.

LEAVE LOVE SYMBOLS
AT HOME

Auspicious symbols like the *mou tan* flower
(or mountain peony) and mandarin ducks
are excellent for the home but can cause
problems in the workplace, so do not display
these romantic energizers at work.

ABOUT THE AUTHOR

Lillian Too has written several bestselling books on feng shui, including *The Complete Illustrated Guide to Feng Shui*, *The Complete Illustrated Guide to Feng Shui For Gardens*, the *Feng Shui Fundamentals* series and *Lillian Too's Little Book of Feng Shui*.

She heads the publishing and investment company that she founded in Malaysia, where she now lives. She is married with one daughter.

Lillian Too's website address is:
www.lillian-too.com

also check out www.worldoffengshui.com
– the first online feng shui magazine

ENERGIZE EARTH CORNERS TO CREATE 'GOLD'

Activate the southwest corner of your office
with brickwork and the northeast corner
with natural crystal. This is an excellent way
of finding first-class employees.